John Jay

The fisheries dispute

A suggestion for its adjustment by abrogating the Convention of 1818.

Second Edition

John Jay

The fisheries dispute
A suggestion for its adjustment by abrogating the Convention of 1818. Second Edition

ISBN/EAN: 9783337174897

Printed in Europe, USA, Canada, Australia, Japan

Cover: Foto ©Andreas Hilbeck / pixelio.de

More available books at **www.hansebooks.com**

THE FISHERIES DISPUTE

A Suggestion for its Adjustment by Abrogating
the Convention of 1818, and Resting on
the Rights and Liberties Defined
in the Treaty of 1783

A LETTER

TO

THE HONOURABLE WILLIAM M. EVARTS

OF THE UNITED STATES SENATE

BY

JOHN JAY

LATE MINISTER TO VIENNA

SECOND EDITION

NEW YORK
DODD, MEAD & COMPANY
PUBLISHERS
1887

THE FISHERIES DISPUTE.

DEAR MR. EVARTS : The necessity of some decisive action by the Government to arrest the vexatious and harassing treatment of our fishermen by the Canadian authorities is recognized by the country, as well for the protection of our own rights as for the avoidance of a breach of our harmonious relations with Great Britain ; and the passage in the Senate by 46 to 1 of Senator Edmunds' bill to authorize the President to protect and defend the rights of American fishing vessels, American fishermen, and American trading and other vessels in certain cases for other purposes, seems to show that the Senate shares the judgment of the country that a continuance of the policy under which such annoyances are possible would be a mistake, and that their further toleration is forbidden by a decent regard to the rights of our fishermen, and to the peace, interest, and dignity of the nation.

Upon the question how far the bill is calculated to disturb our friendly relations with Great Britain, the New York *Herald* reports your views as follows :

Mr. Evarts argued in support of the bill, which he said, was not in the nature of a menace or tending at all in that direction. It was the duty of Congress to take the subject away from local disturbance, irritation, and resentments. So far from the bill tending to war or tending to umbrage, it was intended to have a contrary effect. It was an immediate announcement to the people that they had only to trust their protection, not to personal resentment, but to the Government of the United States, and when the opening summer should bring about the recurrence of the fishing season and of the fishing dangers, the question would be removed from that theatre of collision ; and, if not concluded, it would be under the contract of both governments, in a deliberate consideration of what should be done in order to have stability of intercourse and in order to give stability to the peace and dignity of the two nations, the United States and Great Britain.

I observe an intimation in the papers that some proposition has been made by our Government to which it is awaiting a reply, and I am sensible of the delicacy with which one not thoroughly aware of the state of a negotiation, should venture to offer advice. This question of the fisheries, however, is peculiarly a question for the people, and the recent reports in the Senate and the House, the correspondence on the subject submitted by the President on December 8, 1886, and again on February 8, 1887, with the replies of the Secretary of the Treasury to the House of December 14, 1886, and of February 5, 1887, and the letter of Secretary Bayard to the Senate of January 26, 1887, with the bills proposed by Senator Edmunds and Mr. Belmont, the resolution of Mr. Gorman, and the bill proposed by Secretary Manning, have brought the pending questions so fully before the country, with the facts and correspondence to so late a day, that a suggestion offered for consideration and based upon historic data and recent facts, will hardly I think be regarded as untimely or improper.

RETALIATION AS A REMEDY, TEMPORARY AND INCOMPLETE.

The difficulty which we propose to reach by retaliation seems to arise in great part from a seemingly irreconcilable difference of opinion between the government of Great Britain and that of the United States, touching the extent of the rights of our fishermen under the Convention of 1818. And if that Convention is really the source of the trouble which we have had with intervals during seventy years, is retaliation in truth the most complete and proper remedy ? or may not a threat have upon the English people the effect it would have upon ourselves, disposing us to fight rather than to argue ? or if we are forced to retaliation as a last resort, should not its suggestion be accompanied by some proposition looking to a fundamental and permanent read-justment of our rights ?

When Mr. Bayard, under the date of November 6, 1886, referring to the seizure of the Marion Grimes, held that the Dominion Government was seeking by its action in the matter to " invade and destroy the commercial rights and privileges secured to the citizens of the United States under and by virtue of treaty stipulations with Great Britain," the Governor-General of Canada, the Marquis of Lans-downe held that that statement was " not warranted by the facts of the case," and that the two vessels that had been seized were " fishing vessels and not traders, and therefore liable, subject to the guiding of the courts, to any penal-ties imposed by law for the enforcement of the Convention of 1818, on parties violating the terms of that Conven-tion."

Nor was this simply the judgment of the Governor-Gen-eral of Canada, for Earl Rosebery wrote : " I have to add that Her Majesty's Government entirely concurs in the view expressed by the Marquis of Lansdowne."

If the judgment of the British Government on that point, based apparently on a system of interpretation which is held at Washington to be so narrow, strained, and technical that it ignores not only the motives which induced Ameri-cans to accept the Treaty of 1818, but ignores also the rights and the duties that belong to international comity and the law of nations—if that judgment has not been changed by the able and courteous arguments of Mr. Bayard and Mr. Phelps, and the grave reports of Senator Edmunds and Mr. Manning, is it likely to yield more readily when the calm of diplomacy shall have been interrupted by the irritating measures of retaliation, which Senator Edmunds' bill, or the yet more stringent bill by Mr. Belmont in the House, ex-tending to Canadian locomotives and cars, goods, wares, and merchandise, authorizes the President to proclaim? Will it be more easy to come to an amicable understanding, after the vessels of the British Dominion in America have been excluded from our ports, or Canadian railway trains stopped at the border, in retaliation for the treatment of our fishermen; a treatment which the Ministers of Canada and Great Britain declare is justified by the strict letter of the Treaty of 1818, however, in the eyes of Americans, unfriendly, inhospitable, or even barbarous?

BRITISH MISCONSTRUCTION OF THE TREATY OF 1818.

On one point both Mr. Bayard and Earl Rosebery, Mr. Phelps and Lord Salisbury seem to be agreed, that the Treaty of 1818 is the law on the interpretation of which depends the decision of the question in dispute. But the recent correspondence on the rights of American fishermen, submitted by the President to the Senate on December 8, 1886, shows that this apparently simple question of interpretation is, in the view of the Department, fairly influenced by the series of laws and regulations referred to by Mr. Bayard, affecting the trade between the British Provinces of North America and the United States, which have since been respectively adopted by the two countries, and have led to amicable and beneficial relations between their respective inhabitants, building up a trade between the two countries founded on mutual interest and advantage, and establishing a reciprocal liberty of commerce. The question is next, as Mr. Bayard and Mr. Manning have both shown, improperly subjected, as regards American rights, to acts of colonial legislation under a supposed delegation of jurisdiction by the Imperial Government of Great Britain, and seemingly intended to include authority to interpret and enforce the provisions of the Treaty of 1818. The effect of the colonial legislation and colonial executive interpretation, if executed according to the letter, would be, as Mr. Bayard contends in his letter to Sir L. B. Sackville West,

of May 10, 1886, to expand the restrictions and renuncia-
tions of the Treaty of 1818, and to further diminish and
practically destroy the privileges expressly secured to
American fishing vessels to visit the inshore waters for
shelter, the repair of damages, the purchase of wood, and
the obtaining of water.

The seizure and detention, for instance, by the Canadian
authorities of the David J. Adams, which Mr. Bayard in
his note to Sir Lionel B. Sackville West, of May 20, 1886,
characterized as " unwarranted, irregular, and severe," ap-
peared to rest on charges :

I. Of violating the Treaty of 1818.

II. Of alleged violation of the Act 59 George III.

III. Of alleged violation of the colonial Act of Nova
Scotia of 1818, and

IV. Of alleged violation of Canadian Statutes of 1870
and 1883.

And Mr. Bayard, in his telegram of May 22d, to Mr.
Phelps, refers to " vexatious interpretations, and actions of
local authorities which can only hinder an amicable award."
On June 14th, Secretary Bayard, in regard to the allegations
that American vessels would not be permitted to land fish
at Halifax for transportation in bond across the Province,
and that American vessels had been warned to keep outside
of a line drawn from headland to headland, said :

Against this treatment I must instantly and formally protest as an
unwarrantable interpretation and application of the Treaty by the officers of the Dominion of Canada and the Province of Nova Scotia ; as
an invasion of the laws of commercial and maritime intercourse existing between the two countries, and a violation of hospitality ; and for
any loss or injury resulting therefrom the Government of Her British
Majesty will be held responsible.

In reply to your complaints of outrages, the British Minister at
Washington has advised us that the matter has been referred to the
Dominion Government, and Mr. Phelps at London has been informed
that no further steps can be taken about the cases before the Canadian
courts have been adjudicated.

The question, therefore, of the rights of American fishermen under the Treaty of 1818, is made by the British Government to depend not altogether on that Treaty alone, but
partly, as it would seem, on a statute of George III., on
colonial acts of the British Provinces, the rulings of Canadian courts, and the proclamation and acts of colonial officers—all assuming to be based on the provisions of that
Treaty. This fact justifies a careful consideration of the
relative advantages and disadvantages which result to us at
this moment from the Convention which for so long a time
has played a principal part in this regretable and chronic
controversy—a treaty which under the interpretation placed
upon it by Canadian and British officials is being used not
as a shield to protect our fishermen in the enjoyment of their
rights, but as a weapon for the interruption of their business
and their helpless subjection to wrong and humiliation.

This state of things, which by no means accords with the
American idea of national fitness, and which it is proposed
temporarily to correct if necessary by retaliation, clearly re-
quires a thorough and permanent change, based not on retaliation for wrong, but on clear principles of right; and we
find two propositions from British sources looking to a
peaceful remedy which deserve respectful consideration.

OFFERS OF NEGOTIATION AND ARBITRATION.

The one is a proposition from Lord Rosebery for a frank
and friendly consideration of the whole question with a view
to the revision of the Treaty of 1818.

The second is said to be a semi-official proposition from
the *Montreal Gazette*, the official organ of the Dominion
Government of the 25th of January, which said : " If, instead
of resorting to coercive measures, the United States Congress could consent to ARBITRATION, it would adopt the
manlier and more dignified course."

Either of these plans, adopted by mutual agreement, upon
a basis that would certainly secure the original rights and

interests of our fishermen as recognized by Great Britain in the Treaty of Peace, would be preferable to any measure that might bear the character of opposition or retaliation. But without an admitted basis of principle and right distinctly formulated, as were the three rules laid down for the Geneva Arbitration, and to which Great Britain wisely gave her adhesion, it would seem idle to expect a satisfactory measure of justice either from negotiation or arbitration. Our recent negotiations have only served to make more clear the fact that the two governments look at the rights of our fishermen from different stand-points ; and without an agreement in advance upon the rules by which the arbitrators are to be guided, an award would probably dissatisfy the defeated party, and serve as little to commend arbitration to thoughtful English or Americans as the American claim for indirect damages at Geneva, or the award of the Belgian umpire at Halifax.

There should be no difficulty in agreeing on a basis for either negotiation or arbitration, in the shape of rules declaring the right of our fishermen in language that even our Canadian friends can understand, when it is remembered that their violation of the Treaty of 1818 has given us a right to abrogate that treaty ; and that its abrogation would restore our rights and liberties under Article III. of the Treaty of Peace in 1783, which were renounced and surrendered by the Treaty of 1818, but which would revive were the Treaty of 1818 abrogated ; precisely as the latter treaty, after being suspended by the adoption of the Reciprocity Treaty of 1854, was revived by its termination in 1866 ; and after being again suspended by the Treaty of 1871, was again restored by its termination in 1885. If our British friends should have a doubt upon this point, and be inclined to think that our regard for the sanctity of treaties will induce us to pardon their violation, or that the exploded suggestion that our ancient fishery rights recognized and defined at the peace, were lost by the war of 1812, a glance at the law and the facts, at the testimony of history and the opinions of English lawyers, should easily satisfy them on these points.

THE BRITISH PROPOSITION TO REVISE THE TREATY.

The note of the Earl of Rosebery to Mr. West, under date of July 10, 1886, declining to discuss the competency of the Canadian authorities under the existing statutes, imperial or colonial, to effect the seizure of American vessels complained of, as a question which he says is occupying the courts of law, continues : " I cannot, however, close this despatch without adding that Her Majesty's Government entirely concurs in that passage of the report of the American Privy Council, in which it is observed that ' If the provisions of the Convention of 1818 have become inconvenient to either contracting party the utmost that good-will and fair dealing can suggest is that the terms shall be reconsidered.' " Lord Rosebery adds :

It is assuredly from no fault on the part of Her Majesty's Government that the question has now been relegated to the terms of the Convention of 1818. They have not ceased to express their anxiety to commence negotiations, and *they are now prepared to enter upon a frank and friendly consideration of the whole question, with the most earnest desire to arrive at a settlement consonant alike with the rights and interests of Canada and the United States.*

Does not this suggestion, originating with the Canadian Privy Council and entirely concurred in by Great Britain, point to the fact from which we do not dissent, that the Convention of 1818 lies at the bottom of the difficulties which it is proposed to correct by Presidential proclamation, and that that Convention must be satisfactorily revised, or entirely abrogated, before we can reach a satisfactory and permanent settlement of the fisheries question.

Admitting Lord Rosebery to be in the right in contending that it was from no fault on the part of Her Majesty's Government that the question has been relegated to the terms of the Convention of 1818, and recognizing the frank and friendly assurance of their most earnest desire to arrive at a settlement consonant with the rights and interests of the United States, it will be less easy to defend the British Government from the grave responsibility of having persistently instigated, first at Ghent, and again at London, the adoption of the Article of 1818 by their persistence in the bold assertion, which British law officers had shown to be unsound, that we had lost by the War of 1812 our original and ancient rights to the fisheries as recognized and defined in the Treaty of Peace, and by their acting in advance on that groundless suggestion as soon as the war had closed, by warning and seizing our fishing vessels without reason and without law.

Nothing, therefore, could more become the noblest characteristics of the British Government and the British people, than a frank and practical exhibition of the honorable desire expressed by Lord Rosebery to arrive at a just settlement of the question. If they assent to the abandonment of the Convention of 1818, fraught as it is with errors of law and wrongful acts, and which for two generations has crippled our fishermen in their ancient rights, and subjected the Republic to vexations and affronts which have become so intolerable that the gravest legislative body in the Republic is ready for retaliation ; if they assent to a return to the fair division of the fisheries made by the two empires at the peace of 1783—and when they recall the part borne by Americans, and especially the New Englanders, during two centuries in securing the fisheries, they may well admire the moderation of our demands and the generosity of our concessions—there would seem to be no shadow of reason why the entire question of the fisheries should not be arranged with good-will on all sides ; and with a common disposition to advance in our commercial arrangements the mutual interests of Great Britain, Canada, and the United States.

A glance at the recent treatment of our fishing vessels

will help to show whether there is any reasonable prospect of an amicable arrangement, especially in view of the proposed measures of retaliation, on the basis of the Article of 1818, as interpreted by the British Government, and will exhibit the solid grounds for the belief expressed at Washington that that convention has been directly violated by the British both in legislation and in practice.

THE RECENT TREATMENT OF AMERICAN FISHING VESSELS.

Looking at the correspondence, it would seem as if every attempt on our part for an amicable arrangement had become hopeless through the irreconcilable difference of view as to the rights of Americans under the Treaty of 1818, and an apparent confidence on the part of our Canadian neighbors, which seems to have increased rather than diminished since our payment of the Halifax award, that we have no rights to protect, and no treaty stipulation under which we can claim protection. The peaceful efforts of our Government have been ineffectual, and their just hopes have been disappointed. In April, 1886, Mr. Bayard wrote to Messrs. Cushing and McKennay, of Portland, who had fishing vessels ready for the Banks, and who had asked if their fishing vessels could call at Canadian ports for men and be protected in so doing :   '

. . . I expect to obtain such an understanding as will relieve our fishermen from all doubts or risk in the exercise of the ordinary commercial privileges of friendly ports, to which, under existing laws of both countries, I consider their citizens to be mutually entitled free from molestation. . . .

On July 26, 1886, President Cleveland sent to the Senate a Report of the Secretary of State relating to the seizures and detentions of American vessels in Canadian waters, in which Mr. Bayard referred to the correspondence then pending as one " which it is believed must soon terminate in an amiable settlement mutually just and honorable and therefore satisfactory to both countries and their inhabitants."

But if we look at the correspondence submitted by the President on December 8, 1886, and again on February 8, 1887, we find the treatment of our fishermen more intolerable than ever.

The case of the Rattler, seeking shelter from a storm in the harbor of Shelburne, Nova Scotia, induced Mr. Bayard to say to Mr. Hardinge (August 9, 1886) : " The hospitality which all civilized nations prescribe has thus been violated and THE STIPULATIONS OF A TREATY GROSSLY INFRACTED."

In the case of the Shiloh and Julia Ellen, Mr. Bayard (August 18, 1886) protested " against the hostile and outrageous misbehavior of Captain Quigley, of the Canadian cruiser, Terror," and said, " the firing of a gun across their bows was a most unusual and wholly uncalled-for exhibition of hostility, and equally so was the placing of armed men on board the lawful and peaceful craft of a friendly nation," although Captain Quigley gave another version of his acts. In the case of the " Mollie Adams," whose water-tank had been burst by heavy weather, and whose master was refused permission by the Collector at Port Mulgrave to purchase two or three barrels to hold water on their homeward voyage, the vessel was compelled to put to sea with an insufficient supply of water, and in trying to make another port wherein to obtain it, encountered a gale which swept away a deck-load of fish and two seine boats, and Mr. Bayard (September 10, 1886) denounced the conduct of the custom officer as " inhospitable and inhuman."

Again, September 23, 1886, Mr. Bayard had to complain of the treatment of the A. R. Crittenden, whose master stopped at Steep Creek for water, and was told by the Customs Officer that if he took in water his vessel would be seized, whereupon he sailed without the needed supply, and was obliged to put his men on a short allowance of water during the passage homeward. Mr. Bayard characterized

this conduct as " unlawful and inhuman," and as affording
" an illustration of the very vexatious spirit in which the
officers of the Dominion of Canada appear to seek and pe-
nalize and oppress those fishing vessels of the United States,
lawfully engaged in fishing, which from any cause are
brought within their reach."

On November 6, 1886, Mr. Bayard wrote to Mr. Phelps :

The hospitality of Canadian coasts and harbors, which are ours by
ancient right, and which these treaties confirm, costs Canada nothing,
and are productive of advantages to her people. Yet, in defiance of
the most solemn obligations, in utter disregard of the facilities and
assistances granted by the United States, and in a way especially irritating, a deliberate plan of annoyances and aggressions has been insti-
tuted and plainly exhibited during the last fishing season, a plan calculated to drive these fishermen from shores where, without injury to
others, they prosecute their own legitimate and useful industry.

It is impossible not to see that if the unfriendly and unjust system, of which these cases now presented are a part, is sustained by
Her Majesty's Government, serious results will almost necessarily
ensue, great as the desire of this Government is to maintain the relations of good neighborhood (49th Congress, 2d Session, House of
Representatives, Ex. Doc. 19, p. 160).

The question asked by Mr. Bayard of Sir Lionel West
(May 10, 1886) is still the question before the country :

Whether such a construction is admissible as would convert the
Treaty of 1818, from being an instrumentality for the protection of the
in-shore fisheries along the described parts of the British American
coasts, into a pretext or means of obstructing the business of deep-
sea fishing by citizens of the United States, and of the interrupting and
destroying the commercial intercourse that since the Treaty of 1818,
and independent of any treaty whatever, has grown up and now ex-
ists under the concurrent and friendly laws and mercantile regulations
of the respective countries (42d Congress, 2d Session, House of
Representatives, Ex. Doc., p. 9).

The wide and irreconcilable differences between the view
of American rights under the Treaty of 1818 taken by Mr.
Bayard, Mr. Phelps, and Mr. Senator Edmunds, represent-

ing the Committee on Foreign Relations in the Senate, and by Mr. Belmont, representing the like Committee in the House, and the view of our rights under that treaty taken by the Canadian authorities, and adopted or acquiesced in by the British Government, seem to show the hopelessness of coming to an agreement under that treaty.

The Decided View of Secretary Manning.

The Secretary of the Treasury, Mr. Manning, in his very able response to the Committee on Foreign Affairs in the House of Representatives, dated February 6, 1887, on the fisheries question, says (p. 4) :

It is impossible not to recognize how justly my colleague, Mr. Bayard, has portrayed the inhumanity and brutality with which certain Canadian officials treated defenceless American fishermen during the last summer, even those who had gone out of their way to rescue Canadian sailors, and having entered a Canadian bay to safely land those they had saved, attempted to procure food to sustain their own lives.

Mr. Manning shows that the " restrictions " enforced by Canadian statutes and officials against our fishermen, under pretence of restricting commercial privileges, are, in fact, in violation of our fishing rights and of the Treaty of 1818, and he tells us of a new Canadian Act, approved by the Queen in Council on November 26, 1886, entitled " An Act further to amend the Acts respecting fisheries by foreign vessels," and Mr. Manning says :

The Canadian Act thus having the royal approval was intended, as has been openly avowed, to forfeit any American fishing vessel which is found having entered Canadian waters, or the port of Halifax, to buy ice, bait, or other articles, or for any purpose other than shelter, repairs, wood, or water. That we deny, and reply that such legislation is a repeal and annulment by England of the arrangement made in 1830, and to that repeal we are entitled to respond by a similar repeal of our own law, and by a refusal hereafter, and while debate or negotiation goes on, to confer hospitality or any privilege whatever in our ports on Canadian vessels or boats of any sort. A violation of amity may be looked upon as an unfriendly act, but not a cause for a just war. England may judge for herself of the nature and extent of the amity and courtesy she will show to us. In the present case we do not propose retaliation ; we simply respond—we, too, suspend amity and hospitality.

THE VIEW OF THE SENATE COMMITTEE.

The report of Senator Edmunds on behalf of the Committee on Foreign Relations (49th Congress, 2d Session, Senate Report, No. 1,683, January 19, 1887), after a careful analysis of the treaties and of the British Canadian legislation on the fisheries question, including " An Act further to amend the Acts respecting fisheries by foreign vessels," approved by the Queen in Council, November 26, 1886, commented on by Secretary Manning, and after remarking :

From all this it would seem that it is the deliberate purpose of the British government to leave it to the individual discretion of each one of the numerous subordinate magistrates, fishery officers, and customs officers of the Dominion of Canada to seize and bring into port any American vessels, whether fishing or other, that he finds within any harbor in Canada, or hovering within Canadian waters. The statute does not even except that Canadian waters in which a large part of the southern coast and the whole of the western coast of Newfoundland they are entitled to fish, to say nothing of the vast extent of the continental coast of Canada.

The Committee repeats its expression of the firm opinion *that this legislation is in violation of the Treaty of* 1818, *as it respects American fishing vessels,* and in violation of the principles of amity and good neighborhood that ought to exist in respect of commercial intercourse or the coming of the vessels of either having any commercial character within the waters of the other. Had it been intended to harass and embarrass American fishing and other vessels, and to make impracticable further to enjoy their treaty and other common rights, such legislation would have been perfectly adapted to that end.

With this uniformity of agreement on the point that Great Britain is deliberately violating the treaty of 1818, and withholding the privileges to our fishermen in consideration of which we surrendered our olden rights and liberties in the

Newfoundland fisheries, can we consent with a due regard
to national fitness to any further delays ? Is there any good
reason why we should not notify Great Britain that unless
our rights under the treaty, as we understand them, are at
once recognized and permanently protected, we propose to
abrogate the first article of the Treaty of 1818, as for a similar reason—non-performance of contract—we terminated
in the last century out treaties with France.

ABROGATION OF TREATIES FOR VIOLATION OF CON-
TRACT.

On July 1, 1798, Congress annulled by act the treaties with France made in 1778, stating among the reasons
for the act, that these treaties had been repeatedly violated
on the part of the French Government ; that the just claims
of the United States for reparation of the injuries so committed have been refused, and that there was still pursued
against the United States a system of prevailing violence
infracting the said treaties and hostile to the rights of a
free and independent nation (t U. S. Stat., i., 578 ; Wharton's International Law Digest, 137 a).

The act was sustained by the American envoys, Messrs.
Ellsworth, Davie, and Murray, in a letter to the French en-
voys. July 23, 1800, on the ground of prior violation by
France.

It was remarked that treaties being a mutual compact, a palpa-
ble violation of it by one party did, by the law of nature and of nations, leave it optional with the other to renounce and declare the same
to be no longer obligatory ; and that of necessity there being no common tribunal to which they could appeal, the remaining party must
decide whether there had been such violation on the other part as to
justify renunciation.

To the further suggestion that the laws of nations admitted of a dissolution of treaties only by mutual consent or war, it was remarked by the American envoys
that Vattel in particular, the best approved of modern

2

writers, not only held that a treaty violated by one party
might for that reason be renounced by the other, but that
when there were two treaties between the same parties,
one might be rendered void in that way, and the other remain in force.

Mr. Madison wrote to Mr. Edmund Pendleton, January
2, 1791 (1. Madison's Works, 524) :

That the contracting power can annul the treaty cannot I pre-
sume be questioned, the same authority precisely being exercised in
annulling, as in making a treaty.

That a breach on one side (even of a single article, each being considered as a condition of every other article) *discharges the other, is
as little questionable,* but with this reservation that the other side is at
liberty to take advantage or not of the breach, as dissolving the
treaty. . . .

It is, of course, desirable that whatever disposition is
made of the Fisheries Convention of 1818, which has so long
been a source of trouble, should be made by mutual consent,
and that with its departure the international differences
should cease. But if Great Britain, under whatever influence,
should refuse her assent to this, and if our Government is
satisfied not only that we are entitled to abrogate the treaty,
but that the rights of our citizens and the national dignity
demand its abrogation, a review of historic facts and of the
law of nations applicable to the Treaty of 1783, and of the
opinions of learned crown lawyers of Great Britain and of
distinguished jurists in the United States, all seem to unite in
showing that the abrogation of the first article of the Treaty
of 1818 would revive in full force our original rights as defined in the third article of the Treaty of Peace in 1783.
The article which would be thus restored is as follows :

ARTICLE III.

It is agreed that the people of the United States shall continue to
enjoy unmolested the right to take fish of every kind on the sand bank
and all the other banks of Newfoundland, also in the Gulf of St. Lawrence, and at all other places in the sea, where the inhabitants of both
countries used at any time heretofore to fish.

And also that the inhabitants of the United States shall have liberty to take fish of every kind on such part of the coast of Newfoundland as British fishermen shall use (but not to dry or cure the same on that island), and also on the coasts, bays, and creeks of all other of his Britannic Majesty's Dominions in America ; and that the American fishermen shall have liberty to dry and cure fish in any of the unsettled bays, harbors, and creeks of Nova Scotia, Magdalen Islands, and Labrador, so long as the same shall remain unsettled ; but so soon as the same or either of them shall be settled, it shall not be lawful for the said fishermen to dry or cure fish at such settlements without a previous agreement for that purpose with the inhabitants, proprietors, or possessors of the land.

THE NEWFOUNDLAND FISHERIES IN EUROPEAN AND AMERICAN HISTORY.

Before passing to the unsuccessful attempt of the British Commissioners at Ghent, at the close of the War of 1812, to persuade the American Commissioners that the fisheries article had been abrogated by the war, and to their greater success in London in 1818, when Messrs. Rush and Gallatin voluntarily surrendered our olden rights and consented to the conditions under which our fishermen are now so ill-treated, it may be well to recall some of the principal incidents that preceded and attended the Treaty of Peace, and which explain the regard shown by the old Congress to the value of the fisheries, and the rights of the fishermen : and the difficulties which had to be overcome by the American Commissioners at Paris before they could secure for the young republic the rights and liberties guaranteed by Article III., and which by the Treaty of 1818 were needlessly surrendered.

Senator Edmunds remarked, in the *North American Review*, that "no permanent gain for American interests has been made since the Treaty of 1783." As regards our fishermen, were the technical reasoning of our Canadian neighbors to be accepted as correct, it might be said that American diplomacy had stripped them of their right to decent and hospitable treatment conferred by the law of God, and recognized as sacred by the law of nations.

The history of the Newfoundland fisheries, of which an interesting sketch is given in the learned report of the late Lorenzo Sabine, of Massachusetts, submitted by the Hon. Thomas Corwin, Secretary of the Treasury in 1853, throws light not only upon the estimate of their importance by the American Congress, but by the courts of England, of France, and of Spain.

The Newfoundland fisheries were known to the Biscayans and Normans in 1504, and in 1517 fifty ships of different nations were engaged in them. In 1577, the French employed one hundred and fifty vessels, and by Henry IV., and his great Minister Sully, the Newfoundland cod-fishery was placed under the care of the government, and to her fisheries France was indebted for her possessions in America.

The first difficulties from rival grants of land by France and England occurred in Acadia, which embraced the present colonies of Nova Scotia, and New Brunswick and Maine, between the Kennebec and the St. Croix Rivers. These were limited by the Treaty of St. Germain in 1683, by which Charles I., who had married a French princess, resigned certain places, whose cession was afterward held to be fraudulent by Cromwell, who erected Nova Scotia into a colony, and after the restoration of the Stuarts, by the Treaty of Breda in 1667, it passed a second time to France. A third treaty, that of London in 1686, confirmed the two powers in their respective colonies. On the proclamation of war between England and France on the accession of William and Mary, Massachusetts commenced preparations for the conquest of Nova Scotia and Canada, under Sir William Phipps ; and at the peace of Ryswick, in 1697, Nova Scotia was again returned to the French, who promulgated a claim to the sole ownership of the fisheries, Villabon, Governor of Nova Scotia, notified the Governor of Massachusetts of royal instructions from France to seize

every American fisherman who ventured east of the Kennebec River into Maine, and the historian writes, "On both
sides the strife was for the monopoly and for the mastery."

In 1699 came to Boston the Earl of Bellamont. In the
first year of Queen Anne, the two nations were again at
war, and among the causes were the claims of France to a
part of Maine and the whole of the fishing grounds. The
people of New England engaged heartily in the contest and
equipped a fleet at Boston ; and after a doubtful struggle
in 1710 Nova Scotia became an English province, and the
Home Ministry attempted the conquest of Canada, a
scheme designed by Bolingbroke and mismanaged by a
Commander Hill, who, with troops fresh from the victories
of Marlborough, aided by trained colonists of New England,
lost by wreck in the passage up the St. Lawrence eight
ships and more than eight hundred men.

By the Treaty of Utrecht, in 1713, England obtained the
supremacy and monopoly of the fisheries of our seas, and
the Tory statesmen, headed by Oxford and Bolingbroke, safe
from foreign dangers, quarrelled among themselves. Oxford was impeached for high treason by the House of Commons and committed to the Tower, and among the charges
against him was that Robert Earl of Oxford and Earl Mor-
timer had in defiance of an act of Parliament advised their
Sovereign that "the subjects of France should have the
liberty of fishing and drying fish in Newfoundland." "But
such," wrote the historian, "has been the advance of civilization, and of the doctrine of human brotherhood, that an
act which was a flagrant crime in his own age has become
one honorable to his memory. The great principle he thus
maintained in disgrace, that the seas of British America are
not to be held by British subjects as a monoply, and to the
exclusion of all other people, has never since been wholly
disregarded by any British Minister, and we may hope will
even now appear in British diplomacy to mark the progress
of liberal principles and of man's humanity to man."

The French, undismayed by the loss of Nova Scotia,

settled and fortified Cape Breton, and in 1721 their fleet of
fishing vessels was larger than ever and said to be quite
four hundred.

In 1745 England and France were again at war, and the
conquest of Cape Breton was undertaken, and Louisbourg,
named in honor of the King, was the point of attack—
" twenty-five years and thirty million of livres had been re-
quired to complete it, and more than two hundred cannon
were mounted to defend it. So great was its strength
that it was called ' The Dunkirk of America.' It had nun-
neries and palaces, terraces and gardens. That such a city
rose upon a lone desolate isle in the infancy of American
colonization appears incredible ; explanation is alone found
in the fishing enthusiasm of the period." The fleet sailed
from Boston in March. The colonial ships and the royal
squadron, supported by the colonists on shore, maintained
the siege with surprising energy. Nine thousand cannon-
balls and six hundred bombs were discharged by the assail-
ants, fifteen hundred of whom, badly sheltered and exposed
to cold and fog, became unfit for duty, and yet on the forty-
ninth day of the investment the French commander surrendered, and Pepperell, by keeping the French flag flying,
lured within their grasp ships with cargoes of great value.
Thirty years later the capture was pronounced in the House
of Commons " an everlasting memorial to the zeal, courage,
and perseverance of the troops of New England."

" With the present condition of Cape Breton in view,"
remarks Mr. Sabine, " we almost imagine that we hold in
our hands books of fiction rather than the records of the real,
when we read as we do in Smollett that the conquest of
Louisbourg was ' the most important achievement of the
war of 1744,' and in the Universal History that ' *New England gave peace to Europe* by raising an army and trans-
porting four thousand men, whose success proved an equivalent for all the successes of France on the Continent.' "

By the peace of Aix-la-Chapelle in 1748, which has been
pronounced dishonorable to England at home and in her

colonies, Cape Breton was restored to France, and among
the results of that peace was counted the alienation of the
affection of the people of New England, who felt that the
House of Hanover, like the Stuarts, were ready to sacrifice
their victories and their interests as " equivalents " for de-
feats and disasters in Europe.

In 1756 came another war between Great Britain and
France, and two years later the second siege of Louisbourg
by twenty ships of the line, eighteen frigates, a fleet of smaller
vessels, and an army of fourteen thousand men.   The success of this expedition, in which Wolfe commanded a corps,
caused great rejoicings in England, and the French colours
were deposited at St. Paul's.   In this last war Americans
bore a distinguished part, and it was said in the House of
Commons that of the seamen employed in the British navy
ten thousand were natives of America.   Among the prominent actors were many who became prominent in our revolution.   With Pepperell at Louisbourg were Thornton, a
signer of the Declaration of Independence ; Bradford,
Gridley, who laid out the works on Bunker Hill ; and on the
frontiers of Virginia and in the West was Washington.   Engaged in one or other of the French Wars were Sears, Wol-
cott, Williams, and Livingston, all among the signers ; Pres-
cott, Montgomery, Gates, Mercer, Morgan, Thomas, James
Clinton (the father of DeWitt Clinton), Stark, Spencer, the
Putnams, Nixon, St. Clair, Gibson, Bull, Durke, Butler,
Campbell, and Chief Justice Dyer of Connecticut.   It was,
says Sabine, in Nova Scotia and Canada and Ohio, at Port
Royal, Causeam, Louisbourg, Quebec, and in the wilds of
Virginia, that our fathers acquired the skill and experience
necessary for the successful assertion of our rights.

By the Treaty of Paris in 1763, when Canada and its
dependencies were formally ceded to Great Britain, France
received the right of fishing and drying on the coast of
Newfoundland, as provided by the Treaty of Utrecht, but
at a distance of fifteen leagues from Cape Breton—a concession which was viewed with great displeasure in England.

where it was said that "the fisheries were worth more than all Canada."

When in 1778 a treaty of commerce was made between the United States and France, it was provided by articles IX. and X. that neither party should interfere with the fishing rights enjoyed by the other, a provision which seems to have been forgotten by France when, in April, 1779, she secretly agreed with Spain that if she could drive the British from Newfoundland the fisheries should be shared only with Spain.

The Old Congress on the Fisheries.

The historic and memorable part born by the American colonists in securing for Great Britain the Newfoundland fisheries, added to their importance to the colonies themselves, naturally led to a just appreciation of their value.

On October 22, 1778, Congress adopted a plan which is referred to in the instructions given to Franklin "for reducing the Province of Canada," and the first reason given for declaring the reduction of Halifax and Quebec objects of the highest importance, was that "the fishery of Newfoundland is justly considered as the basis of a good Marine" (II. Secret Journal of Congress, 114). On May 27, 1779, it was recorded, on motion of Mr. Burke, seconded by Mr. Douglas, "that in no case by any Treaty of Peace the common right of fishing be given up;" and on June 24, 1779, they voted, "that it is essential to the welfare of all the United States that the inhabitants thereof, at the expiration of the war, should continue to enjoy the free and undisturbed exercise of their common right to fish on the banks of Newfoundland and the other fishing banks and seas of North America" (Do., p. 184).

The earnestness of Congress in this view appears from a further resolution, July 1st, for an explanatory note to the Minister at the Court of Versailles, whereby such common right shall be more explicitly guaranteed. On July 17th, 1779, touching the treaty with England, and on July 29, in

a resolution of which the spirit will be approved by our
harried fishermen of to-day, on motion of Mr. McKean, seconded by Mr. Huntington, it was resolved, that if after a
treaty of peace with Great Britain she shall molest the citizens or inhabitants of any of the United States in taking
fish on the banks and places described in the resolutions
passed on the 22d day of July instant, such molestation
(being in the opinion of Congress a direct violation and
breach of the peace) shall be a common cause of the said
States, and the force of the Union be exerted to obtain re-
dress for the parties injured.

Elaborate reports on the common right of the States to
the fisheries, on January 8, and August 16, 1782 (III.
Secret Journal of Congress, pp. 151, 161), show how thoroughly the subject had been studied.

As regards its instructions Congress, under the influence
of M. Gerard and M. de la Luzerne, the French Ministers at
Philadelphia, took a lower tone when, on June 15, 1781,
it gave to its peace commissioners the humiliating and incredible instruction, which Madison denounced as "a sacrifice of the national dignity," to undertake nothing in the
negotiations for peace or truce without the knowledge and
concurrence of the Ministers of the King of France, "and
ultimately to govern yourselves by their advice and opinion" (X. Diplomatic Correspondence, 75, 76).

While no satisfactory explanation has been given for
the adoption by Congress of this instruction, the reasons
for its being urged by the Court of France have been re-
cently made quite clear by the valuable confidential correspondence of the Count de Vergennes with his agents at
Madrid, Philadelphia, and London, published in part by
the Count de Circourt, and more largely comprised in the
invaluable collection of papers relating to the peace negotiations made by Mr. B. F. Stevens, and now awaiting in
the State Department at Washington the action of the
Government.

M. de Circourt's third volume and the recent " Life of

Lord Shelburne," by his grandson Lord Edmond Fitzmaurice, a brother of Lord Lansdowne, the Governor-General of Canada, both published in 1876, the first at Paris and the second in London, show precisely the position occupied by each of these three powers, Great Britain, France, and Spain, in opposition to the American claims to the fisheries.

THE OPPOSITION OF ENGLAND, FRANCE, AND SPAIN.

England's hostile position on the fisheries was defined by the announcement of the Shelburne Ministry to Mr. Oswald, that " the limit of Canada would, under no circumstances, be made narrower than under the Parliament of 1763, and that the right of drying fish on the shores of Newfoundland could not be conceded to the American fisherman " (III. " Life of Shelburne," p. 255).

When France, by the Treaty of Madrid, April 12, 1779, induced Spain to join in the war against Great Britain, the reluctance of Spain to assist in the independence of revolted colonies, whose power and influence she hated and feared, was overcome by an agreement on the part of France, with small regard to the interests of the United States or to her treaty obligations with the Republic, first, that if the British should be driven from Newfoundland its fisheries were to be shared only with Spain ; and second, that Spain should be left free to exact, as the price of her alliance in the war, a renunciation of every part of the basin of the St. Lawrence and the lakes, and the navigation of the Mississippi, and of all the land between that river and the Alleghanies (X. Bancroft, 190, quoting authorities).

In pursuance of that agreement, and with a view to facilitate the designs of Spain against America to which France had assented, M. de Vergennes gave repeated and elaborate instructions to his diplomatic agents in America. The very ingenious argument of his Excellency against our right to the fisheries is interesting from its complete contrast to the view held by our own Commissioners, and which, as the treaty shows, was, in that solemn instrument, recognized and adopted by the British Government. He said in a letter to M. de la Luzerne, the French Minister at Philadelphia, dated Versailles, September 25, 1777 :

It is essential to remark that the fisheries belong, and have always belonged, to the Crown of Great Britain, and that it was as subjects of the Crown the Americans enjoyed them—consequently, from the moment when they shook off the English yoke and declared themselves independent, they broke the community which existed between them and the metropolis ; and voluntarily relinquished all the advantages which they derived from that community, just as they despoiled England of all the advantages she derived from their union with her.

This is virtually the same argument held by Lord Bathurst in his correspondence with Mr. John Quincy Adams, and by the English Commissioners at Ghent, that " when the Americans by their separation from Great Britain became released from the duties, they became excluded also from the privileges of British subjects."

It should therefore, argued the Count de Vergennes, be well established that from the moment when the colonies published their Declaration of Independence they have ceased to own a share in the fisheries, because they have forfeited by their own act the qualification which entitled them to such a share ; that consequently they can offer to the court of London neither title nor actual possession, from this comes another result, viz., that the Americans having no right to the fishing we can give them no guarantee on that head (III. de Circourt, pp. 276, 277).

This argument conveniently accords with the suggestion which closes the remarkable memoir on the principal object of negotiation for peace given by M. de Circourt (III., pp. 29, 38) from the French archives, that it would be for the interest of England to have the French as companions at Newfoundland rather than the Americans, and agrees with the strong opinion presented to Lords Shelburne and Grantham by M. Reyneval, during his secret visit to Eng-

land in September, 1782, against our right to the fisheries
(III. Shelburne's Life, p. 263).

There would have been more force in the Count's argument had he succeeded in his attempt to induce the American
Commissioners to negotiate under the first commission to
Mr. Oswald, authorizing him to treat with representatives
of "the Thirteen Colonies or plantations." The Count then
argued against an acknowledgment of our independence in
advance of the treaty which would concede it, on the
ground that "it would not be reasonable to expect the effect before the cause," and he told the English Minister
Fitzherbert that the commission would do. Had the
American Commissioners adopted that advice and consented to treat under that designation, their consent might
have given color to his suggestion, that any grant by Great
Britain to her colonies in revolt, of the fisheries or the
boundaries, had been given and accepted as a concession.

The Count's advice, though concurred in by Dr. Franklin, struck Jay as singular, and the refusal of Jay to treat
except on an equal footing stayed for some six weeks the
progress of the negotiations for a general peace, until the
mission of Vaughan, and the considerations of which he
was the bearer, convinced the British Cabinet and brought
the new Commission to Oswald, to treat with "The United
States of America" (Jay to Secretary Livingston, November 17, 1782, VIII. Diplom. Corresp., pp. 135, 141,
200). Then the negotiations commenced between the two
independent and equal powers, and this fact enabled John
Adams to say, nearly forty years afterward—in a letter to
William Thomas, dated August 10, 1822, in a pithy expression which contains a world of thought and of argument,
and which should be borne in mind by the statesmen of both
countries in considering the fishery question : "We considered that treaty as A DIVISION OF THE EMPIRE. Our
independence, our rights to territory and to the fisheries as
practised before the Revolution, were no more a grant from
Britain to us than the treaty was a grant from us of Canada,

Nova Scotia, England, Scotland, and Ireland to the Britons.
The treaty was nothing more than mutual acknowledg-
ment of *antecedent rights*" (August 10, 1882, X. Adams'
Works, 404).

It was fitly called by an English judge "A Treaty of
Separation."

THE FISHERIES CLAUSE A CONDITION OF THE PEACE.

Vaughan's Mission to Shelburne.

The sketches afforded by the official correspondence of
our Commissioners for Peace, and by the diary of Mr. Adams, and the new and most important light thrown upon
the whole subject by the confidential documents from the
French Archives, and by the interesting disclosures in the
Life of Lord Shelburne all confirm this view.

To the latter work we are indebted for the most exact
information we have yet had of the attempt of M. de Rayneval in his secret mission to engage the support of Great
Britain to the French and Spanish scheme. in which those
courts united at the date of their treaty. April, 1779. to deprive the United States of the fisheries, and so to cripple
her boundaries and resources as to confine her to a narrow
strip along the Atlantic, as shown in the map " of North
America, showing the Boundaries of the United States,
Canada, and the Spanish Possessions, according to the pro-
posals of the Court of France, in 1882 " (III. Shelburne's
Life, p. 170). Their limits, according to the secret memoir
given by de Circourt (III., pp. 34, 38), were to be detailed
and " circumscribed with the greatest exactness, and all the
belligerent powers (especially England, France, and Spain)
must bind themselves to prevent any transgression of them."

To Lord Edmond Fitzmaurice, the grandson and biog-
rapher of Lord Shelburne, we are also indebted for the first
account of the full effect of the secret mission of Mr. Benjamin Vaughan, who had been promptly despatched by Jay
to counteract the unfriendly designs of the French envoy,

and apart from its general interest as showing the complete
success of Vaughan's mission in deciding the policy of the
British cabinet in favor of the United States, and in over-
throwing at a blow the scheme for the permanent enfeeble-
ment of the new Republic, in which France and Spain had
been for years united, and to accomplish which their ablest
diplomatists were engaged in Madrid and Paris, at Philadelphia and London, it has a direct bearing on the fisheries
question of to-day, in showing that the British cabinet then
adopted their new policy of conciliation with a complete
advisement that without a recognition of our right to the
fisheries no peace was possible. The " Considerations " submitted by Mr. Vaughan to Lord Shelburne (VIII. Diplomatic
Correspondence, pp. 165, 168) as worthy of attention if
England expected other advantages from peace than a mere
suspension of hostilities, if she looked forward to cordiality,
confidence, and commerce, after touching upon the importance of treating with us on an equal footing, notwithstanding the policy of France to postpone the acknowledgment
of our independence to the conclusion of a general peace,
discussed with perfect frankness the true policy of Great
Britain as regards the fisheries and the boundaries, and said
in conclusion, " that it certainly could not be wise in Britain,
whatever it might be in other nations, thus to sow the seeds
of future war in the very treaty of peace, or to lay in it the
foundation of such distrust and jealousies as on the one
hand would forever prevent confidence and real friendship,
and on the other naturally lead us to strengthen our security
by intimate and permanent alliances with other nations."

In regard to the fisheries the " Considerations " said
" that it would not be wise in Great Britain to think of
dividing the fishery with France and excluding us, because
we could not make peace at such an expense, and because
such an attempt would irritate America still more ; would
perpetuate her resentment, and induce her to use every
possible means of retaliation, and by imposing the most
rigid restraints upon a commerce with Great Britain."

The effect of Vaughan's arrival with these considerations "almost simultaneously with Rayneval" was decisive. The Cabinet at once decided to accept the American proposition as to the commission of Oswald, and to adopt the American policy as opposed to that of France and Spain. The new commission was made out at once and despatched by Vaughan, and Lord Shelburne wrote to Oswald, September 23, 1782—"Having said and done everything which has been desired, there is nothing for me to trouble you with, except to add that we have put the greatest confidence, I believe, ever placed in man in the American Commissioners" (III. Shelburne, pp. 267, 268).

THE NEGOTIATION AT PARIS.—MR. ADAMS' DIARY.

An extract from Mr. Adams' diary, showing what was said and agreed to on both sides about the fisheries the day before the signing of the Provisional Articles, November 29, 1782, throws light upon the intention of both parties, and conclusively answers the attempt of the British Commissioners, at Ghent and London, to show that the Fisheries Article had been annulled by the War of 1812 :

29th, Friday.—Met Mr. Fitzherbert, Mr. Oswald, Mr. Franklin, Mr. Jay, Mr. Laurens, and Mr. Strachey, at Mr. Jay's, *Hotel d'Orleans*, and spent the whole day in discussion about the fisheries and the Tories. I proposed a new article concerning the fishery. It was discussed and turned in every light, and multitudes of amendments proposed on each side ; and at last the article drawn as it was finally agreed to.

The other English gentlemen being withdrawn on some occasion, I asked Mr. Oswald if he could consent to leave out the limitation of three leagues from all their shores and the fifteen from those of Louisburg. He said in his own opinion he was for it ; but his instructions were such that he could not do it. I perceived by this and by several incidents and little circumstances before, which I had remarked to my colleagues, who are much of the same opinion, that Mr. Oswald had an instruction not to settle the articles of the fisheries and refugees without the concurrence of Mr. Fitzherbert and Mr. Strachey.

Upon the return of the other gentlemen, Mr. Strachey proposed to leave out the word " right " of fishing and make it " liberty." Mr. Fitzherbert said that the word right was an obnoxious expression. Upon this I rose up and said : " Gentlemen, is there or can there be a clearer right ? In former treaties—that of Utrecht and that of Paris —France and England have claimed the right and used the word. When God Almighty made the banks of Newfoundland, at three hundred leagues distance from the people of America, and at six hundred leagues distance from those of France and England, did He not give as good a right to the former as to the latter ? If Heaven, as the Creator, gave a right, it is ours at least as much as yours. If occupation and possession give a right, we have it as clearly as you. If war and blood and treasure give a right, ours is as good as yours. We have been continuously fighting in Canada, Cape Breton, and Nova Scotia for the defence of this fishery, and have expended beyond all proportion more than you ; if the right cannot then be denied, why should it not be acknowledged and put out of dispute. Why should we leave room for illiterate fishermen to wrangle and chicane ? " Mr. Fitzherbert said : " The argument is in your favor. I must confess your reasons appear to be good, but Mr. Oswald's instructions were such that he did not see how he could agree with us. . . ." After hearing all this, Mr. Fitzherbert, Mr. Oswald, and Mr. Strachey retired for some time ; and returning, Mr. Fitzherbert said that, upon consulting together and weighing everything as maturely as possible, Mr. Strachey and himself had determined to advise Mr. Oswald to strike with us according to the terms we had proposed as our ultimatum respecting the fishery and the loyalists. Accordingly, we all sat down and read over the whole treaty and corrected it, and agreed to meet to-morrow at Mr. Oswald's house to sign and seal the treaties, which the secretaries would copy fair in the meantime.

I forgot to mention that when we were upon the fishery, and Mr. Strachey and Mr. Fitzherbert were urging us to leave out the word " right " and substitute " liberty," I told them at last, in answer to their proposal, to agree upon all other articles and leave that of the fishery to be adjusted at the definitive treaty. I never could put my hands to any article without satisfaction about the fishery ; that Congress had, three or four years ago, when they did me the honor to give me a commission to make a Treaty of Commerce with Great Britain, given me a positive instruction not to make any such treaty without an article in the Treaty of Peace acknowledging a right to the fishery ; that I was happy that Mr. Laurens was now present, who, I believe, was in Congress at the time and must remember it. Mr. Laurens upon this said, with great firmness, that he was in the same case, and could never give his voice for any articles without this. Mr. Jay spoke up and said it could not be a peace, it would be only an insidious truce without it (III. John Adams' Works, 333, 335).

To this may be properly added an explanatory statement by Mr. Adams in regard to the subsequent substitution of the word liberty for right in parts of the article. He wrote to Mr. Thomas :

That third article was demanded as an *ultimatum*, and it was declared that no Treaty of Peace should ever be made without it ; and when the British Ministers found that peace could not be made without that Article, they consented ; for Britain wanted peace, if possible, more than we did.

We demanded it as a right, and we demanded an explicit acknowledgment of that as an indispensable condition of peace ; and the word right was in the article as agreed to by the British Ministers, but they afterward requested that the word *liberty* might be substituted instead of *right*. They said it amounted to the same thing, for liberty was right, and privilege was right, but the word *right* might be more unpleasant to the people of England than *liberty*: and we did not think it necessary to contend for a word (X. Adams' Works, 404).

The American Commissioners, while yielding to the request of the British Commissioners, may have thought that while the word *liberty* in the context was equivalent to *right*, there was a certain fitness in the proposed substitution, on the ground that while *right* was used in reference to the sea fishery, the word *liberty* might seem more applicable to the fisheries on the coast retained y Britain. This idea was conveyed by Mr. John Quincy Adams, when he said :

At the same moment and by the same act with which the United States acknowledges those coasts and shores as being under a foreign jurisdiction, Great Britain recognized the *liberty* of the people of the United States to use them for purposes connected with the fisheries.

John Adams' statement and argument on this point is confirmed by the fact that the right of fishery, as discussed in Congress and demanded by the American Commissioners

3

as a condition of peace, was not simply the right of taking fish on the banks of Newfoundland, the Gulf of St. Lawrence, and other places in the sea, but the full fishery right, liberty, or privilege—by whatever name it might be called—given by the article, and essential to make their olden enjoyment of the fisheries continuous and complete.

The Stevens' collection of papers bearing on the Peace Negotiations, from the Archives of France and the State Paper Office of London, which, by the courtesy of Mr. Stevens and Mr. Dwight, I had the opportunity of partially examining at the State Department, contains letters from the English Commissioners which fully confirm Mr. Adams' statement that *the entire article* was a condition of peace ; and they show that the English Commissioners were doubtful of the extent of their instructions, and were not quite sure how the treaty, which in fact brought about the downfall of the ministry, would be received in England.

Mr. Strachey to Mr. Thomas Townsend, Paris, November 20th. Eleven at night. " The article of the fishery has been particularly difficult to settle as we thought the instructions were rather limited. It is, however, beyond a doubt that *there could have been no treaty at all if we had not adopted the article as it now stands.*"

Mr. Oswald to Mr. Thomas Townsend, Paris, November 30, 1782. " If we had not given way in the article of the fishery we should have had no treaty at all, Mr. Adams having declared that he would never put his hand to any treaty if the restraints regarding the three leagues and fifteen leagues were not dispensed with, as well as that denying his countrymen the privilege of drying fish on the unsettled parts of Newfoundland."

As the Americans made the entire article a condition of peace, and the English Commissioners assented to it with that understanding, the conclusion seems reasonable, if not irresistible, that as the article was treated as one by them, it should have been treated as one by all who had to do with it, as determining the relative rights and privileges of the two powers in the fisheries, in a division of sovereignty which was intended to be not transient but permanent.

The essential facts of the negotiation on this point mentioned by Mr. Adams, and their striking confirmation by the letters of Mr. Strachey and Mr. Oswald, in the collection of Mr. Stevens, were probably unknown to the commissioners at Ghent; and it is interesting to see how complete an answer they furnish to the very ingenious and plausible arguments of Lord Bathurst in his correspondence with Mr. John Quincy Adams (October 30, 1815)—arguments that were repeated three years later by the English Commissioners at London (Dana's Wheaton).

The *rights* acknowledged by the Treaty of 1783 were not only distinguishable from the liberties conceded by the same Treaty in the foundation on which they stand, but they are carefully distinguished in the wording of the Treaty.

. . . In the Third Article Great Britain acknowledged the right of the United States to take fish on the banks of Newfoundland and other places from which Great Britain had no right to exclude any individual nation, but they were to have the *liberty* to cure and dry them in certain unsettled places within the British territory. If the liberties thus granted were to be as perpetual and indefinite as the right previously recognized, it was difficult to conceive a variation of language so adapted to produce a different impression, and above all, that they should have admitted so strange a restriction of a perpetual and indefinite right as those with which the Article concluded, which left a right so practical and so beneficial as this was admitted to be, dependent on the will of British subjects, proprietors, or possessors of the soil to prohibit its exercise altogether.

It was therefore surely obvious that the word *right* was, throughout the Treaty, used as applicable to what the United States were to enjoy in virtue of a recognized independence ; and the word *liberty* to what they were to enjoy as concessions strictly dependent on the Treaty itself (quoted in Dana's Wheaton, sec. 272).

The point insisted on by Lord Bathurst, that the right of the United States, acknowledged by England, to take fish on the Banks and other places from which Great Britain could not exclude any nation, shows that that clause was not the gist or essence of the Third Article, which the

Americans demanded as the condition of peace, for consenting to which the English Commissioners justified themselves by the declaration that there could be no treaty without it. The change of the word right to liberty, at the urgent request of the English Commissioners, doubtful of their authority and fearful as to the result, on the ground that *liberty* was *right*, and that the change was therefore immaterial, but that the word liberty might be less unpleasant to the people of England, can be easily understood when we read their letters. The American Commissioners had neither doubt nor fear in regard to their share in the treaty. They knew that they had successfully maintained the rights, the boundaries, and the resources of the Republic against the most astute diplomatists of Europe, and had laid the foundation of a lasting peace which, as Hamilton wrote, surpassed, in the excellence of its terms, the expectations of the most sanguine.

"A few hours ago," wrote Oswald to Shelburne (November 29, 1782), "we thought it impossible that any treaty could be made." "If," wrote Strachey to Nepean, "this is not as good a peace as was expected, I am confident it is the best that could have been made. Now, are we to be hanged or applauded for thus rescuing England from the American war?" (III. Shelburne's Life, by Lord Edmund Fitzmaurice, pp. 302, 303).

That the English Commissioners at Paris, Mr. Oswald, Mr. Strachey, and Mr. Fitzherbert, afterward Lord St. Helens, to whose great ability and distinguished services in the negotiation the State-paper Office affords ample tributes, were entirely correct in contending that the word *liberty* might be substituted for *right*, for the reason that it would amount to the same thing, was significantly shown in the Parliamentary debates on the Treaty by the ablest publicists of England, and it is interesting to mark the argument that, what we had enjoyed only as a privilege as Colonists, had become an unlimited right by the Treaty.

In the House of Lords, Lord Loughboro said :

The fishery on the shores retained by Britain is in the next Article *not ceded*, but recognized as A RIGHT inherent in the Americans, which, though no longer British subjects, they are *to continue to enjoy unmolested.*

Here the *liberty* of fishing which Lord Bathurst and Lord Gambier sought to show was a liberty conceded, not a right acknowledged, was pronounced by the Great Chancellor to be "*not ceded*, but recognized as a right inherent in the Americans," and to be enjoyed by them unmolested.

THE TREATY OF GHENT.

No change in the matter of the fisheries was made by the Treaty of Ghent, which was signed on December 24, 1814, by Lord Gambier, Henry Goulburne, and Dr. William Adams, on the part of Great Britain ; and by John Quincy Adams, J. A. Bayard, Jonathan Russell, and Albert Gallatin, on the part of the United States.

Mr. Gallatin wrote to the Secretary of State, with the Treaty : " If according to the construction of the Treaty of 1783, which we assumed, the right was not abrogated by the war, it remains entire, since we most explicitly refused to renounce it either directly or indirectly." Mr. Adams said of the English Commissioners : " Their efforts to obtain our acquiescence in their pretensions that the fishing liberties had been forfeited by the war were unwearied. They presented it to us in every form that ingenuity could desire. It was the first stumbling-block and the last obstacle to the conclusion of the Treaty " (quoted in Sabine's Report on the Principal Fisheries of the American Seas. p. 161. Washington, 1853).

The British government revived the pretence after the conclusion of the Treaty, and the Canadian government presently began to warn and harass our fishermen, and some fishing-vessels were captured.

On March 3, 1815, John Adams wrote a letter of singular vigor to William Cranch from Quincy. He says :

> Our fisheries have not been abandoned. They cannot be abandoned. They shall not be abandoned. We hold them by no grant, gift, bargain, sale, or last will and testament, nor by hereditary descent from Great Britain. We hold them in truth not as kings and priests claim their rights and power, by hypocrisy and craft, but from God and our own swords. . . . We have all the rights and liberties of Englishmen in the fisheries in as full and ample a manner as we had before the Revolution ; we have never forfeited, surrendered, alienated or lost any one punctilio of those rights and liberties ; on the contrary, we compelled the British nation to acknowledge them in the most solemn manner in the Treaty of Peace of 1783.

Mr. Adams then insisted with his sturdy common-sense that we had a stronger, clearer, and more perfect right than the Britons or any other nation of Europe or on the globe, for they were all indebted to us and our ancestors for all these fisheries. " We discovered them, we explored them, we discovered and settled the countries round about them at our own expense, labor, risk, and industry, without assistance from Britain. We have possessed, occupied, exercised and practised them from the beginning. . . .

" If conquest can confer any right, our right is at least equal and common with Englishmen in any part of the world. Indeed, it is incomparably superior, for we conquered all the countries about the fisheries ; we conquered Cape Breton, Nova Scotia, and dispossessed the French, both hostile and neutral."

In conclusion, Mr. Adams declared that the article in the Treaty of 1783 was still in force, and added, " I say it is an acknowledgment not only of an antecedent right, it is of eternal obligation " (X. Adams' Works, 131-133).

According to Mr. Rush the difference of opinion in regard to the fisheries had in 1818 risen to a considerable height, and the United States wholly dissented from the doctrine advanced by the British Commissioners, that the

Treaty of 1783, not being re-enacted or confirmed by the Treaty of Ghent, was annulled by the War of 1812. They insisted that the treaty, after a seven years' contest, made two empires out of one ; that the entire instrument implied permanence—the use of the word *right* in one place and *liberty* in another could make no difference ; that a right of unlimited duration secured by so solemn a deed was as much a right as if stipulated by any other term. Liberty might have seemed a more appropriate term where an enjoyment was guaranteed to one party of a *thing* adjoining territory allotted to the other, but it took nothing from the permanency of the allotment. In point of principle the United States was pre-eminently entitled to all the fisheries, and the restriction at the close of the article stamped permanence upon it. The Treaty of 1783 was altogether unlike common treaties. It contemplated a permanent division of coequal rights, not a transient grant of mere privileges ; the acknowledgment of independence, the establishment of boundaries, and the guarantee of the fisheries each rested upon the same illimitable basis. According to Mr. Rush neither side yielded its conviction to the reasoning of the other, and this being exhausted, there was no resource left with nations disposed to peace but a compromise, and the result was the first article of the Treaty of 1818, under which have arisen the troubles which we have made such fruitless efforts to escape.

THE FISHERIES CONVENTION OF 1818.

Whereas, Differences have arisen respecting the liberty claimed by the United States for the inhabitants thereof to take, dry, and cure fish on certain coasts, bays, harbors, and creeks of His Britannic Majesty's dominions in America, it is agreed between the high contracting parties that

" ARTICLE I.—The inhabitants of the United States shall have forever, in common with the subjects of His Britannic Majesty, the liberty to take fish of every kind on that part of the southern coast of Newfoundland which extends from Cape Ray to the Rameau Islands,

on the western and southern coasts of Newfoundland from the said
Cape Ray to the Quisson Islands, on the shores of the Magdalen Islands, and also on the coasts, bays, harbors, and creeks from Mount
Joly on the southern coast of Labrador, to and through the straits of
Belle Isle, and thence northwardly indefinitely along the coast, without
prejudice, however, to any of the exclusive rights of the Hudson Bay
Company ; and that the American fishermen shall have liberty forever
to dry and cure fish in any of the unsettled bays, harbors, and creeks
of the southern part of the coast of Newfoundland, above described,
and of the coast of Labrador ; but so soon as the same, or any portion
thereof, shall be settled, it shall not be lawful for the said fishermen
to dry or cure fish at such portion so settled without previous agreement for such purpose with the inhabitants, proprietors, or possessors
of the ground. And the United States hereby renounce forever any
liberty heretofore enjoyed or claimed by the inhabitants thereof to
take, dry, or cure fish on or within three marine miles of any of the
coasts, bays, creeks, or harbors of His Britannic Majesty's dominions
in America not included within the above-mentioned limits : PRO-
VIDED, HOWEVER, that the American fishermen shall be admitted to
enter such bays or harbors for the purpose of shelter and of repairing
damages therein, of purchasing wood, and of obtaining water, and for
no other purpose whatever. But they shall be under such restrictions
as may be necessary to prevent their taking, drying, or curing fish
therein, or in any other manner whatever abusing the privileges hereby
reserved to them."

The complications and misunderstandings that arose
under this convention threatened the peace of the two nations, and by the Treaty of 1854, made by Mr. Marcy and
Lord Elgin, the first article of which recited that the liberty
it granted was "in addition to the liberty secured to the
United States fishermen by the convention of October 20,
1818," we temporarily recovered the enjoyment of some of
our ancient rights recognized and continued by the Treaty
of 1783 ; the consideration given on our part being a reciprocity of fishing liberty, and of trade in certain articles
supposed to be greatly to the benefit of Canada. This
treaty was terminated on our notice in 1866, throwing us
back as Great Britain contended, and as we have admitted,
on the Treaty of 1818. Then came the Treaty of 1871, giv-
ing us the right to fish in-shore under certain limitations,

and this, after the rejection by the Senate on February 2, 1875, of another reciprocity treaty, was terminated by our act on July 1, 1885, bringing again into operation the fisheries article of 1818.

Last came the Treaty of Washington, with its mutual grants in regard to the fisheries and trade, and the memorable Article XXII., commencing. "Inasmuch as it is asserted by the government of Her Britannic Majesty that the privileges accorded to the citizens of the United States, under Article XVIII. of this treaty, are of greater value than those accorded by Articles XIX. and XXI. of this treaty to the subjects of Her Britannic Majesty, and this assertion is not admitted by the Government of the United States, it is further agreed," etc., and then followed the provision for commissioners, not to ascertain whether there was in fact an inequality of advantage, and if so which side had received the largest advantage, and to what amount, and which should pay the other for the difference, but to determine the amount of any compensation which in their opinion ought to be paid by the Government of the United States to the government of Her Britannic Majesty in return for the privileges accorded to the citizens of the United States under Article XVIII.

The advantage gained by Great Britain in this form of submission to the commissioners was emphasized by the joint instruction to the Count Beust, by whom, as the Austrian Ambassador at London, the umpire was to be selected, that the appointment of the Minister of Belgium at Washington would be acceptable, not simply to the government of Great Britain, but to that of the United States. Why it had become acceptable to President Grant and his Cabinet has never been explained : but to one suggestion of Mr. Blaine, by way of explanation and apology, made in his interesting sketch of the fisheries dispute from 1818 to 1878, I may properly allude in passing. Mr. Blaine intimates that it was realized at Washington "that Count Von Beust, the Austrian Ambassador, might select some one

even more objectionable than M. Delfosse, if that were
possible." *

From my official and personal relations at Vienna with
the late Chancellor Von Beust I feel bound to say that this
extraordinary and dishonoring suggestion does the greatest
injustice to the character and fame of that illustrious statesman, whose eminent success, aided by the Count Andrassy
at Pesth, in restoring the harmony of Austria and Hungary,
and in introducing into the government of the dual empire
changes in the direction of freedom, education, and national
progress, was not a little influenced by his careful study of
American principles and American institutions, and entitles
his memory to the sincere regard of the American people.

The suggestion that Count Beust, as the Austro-Hunga-
rian Ambassador in London, charged with the appointment of a proper person as umpire in the Halifax award,
would of his own motion have selected a diplomatic agent,
to whom the United States had formally objected, and whom
Earl de Grey had declined to name as one supposed to be
incapacitated by the treaty arrangements between Belgium
and Great Britain, is one entirely inconsistent, not only
with the Count's character and with his friendship to America, as shown in the Naturalization Treaty, but especially
with his regard for diplomatic propriety and his own fame.
So great a breach of faith toward a trustful government
would have been condemned by every court in Europe,
and by honorable diplomatists throughout the world.

The award by the Belgium minister of $5,500,000, in
addition to the duties remitted by us estimated at $4,200,-
000, in the face of the unimpeachable evidence cited by Mr.
Secretary Evarts in his despatch of September 27, 1878,
seems to have been regarded in England as a signal tri-
umph for British and Canadian diplomacy. The prompt
payment of that award was approved by the American
people notwithstanding the rule laid down by Vattel
that " if the arbitrators by pronouncing a sentence evidently

* Twenty Years of Congress, II., 630.

unjust and unreasonable should forfeit the character with which they are invested, their judgment would deserve no attention ; " but that singular award and the steps which led to it may help to explain American reluctance, should any be exhibited, to further arbitration on the fisheries question.

THE EFFECT OF WAR ON TREATIES.

Having referred to the facts which show the intention of the high contracting parties in 1783, that the article on the fisheries in the Treaty of Separation reciting their division between the two empires should not be temporary and transient, but fundamental, permanent, and enduring, and that the acceptance of that article by the British cabinet was a condition of the peace—facts long since established on the American side by the testimony of our own archives, and now confirmed by the letters of the English negotiators gathered after a hundred years from the State Paper Office of London—it may be proper to refer to the simple rule of law, which should determine the question whether that article could be abrogated, as the British commissioners contended, by the War of 1812.

That rule is thus stated in Field's International Code :

TREATIES UNAFFECTED BY WAR.

War does not affect the compacts of a nation except when so provided in such contracts ; and except also that executory stipulations in a special compact between belligerents, which by their nature are applicable only in time of peace, are suspended during the war.

Wharton says :

Treaties stipulating for a permanent arrangement of territorial *and other national rights* are at the most suspended during war, and revive at peace, unless they are waived by the parties, or new and repugnant stipulations are made (II. Wharton's International Law Digest, Chapter VI., Sec. 135).

A large and looser rule was contended for in Society *vs.*
New Haven in the Supreme Court of the United States
in 1823, and the Court was asked to recognize the doctrine
urged at the bar, that treaties become extinguished *ipso*
facto by a war between two governments. But the Court
said, by Justice Washington :

> Whatever may be the latitude of doctrine laid down by element-
> ary writers on the law of nations, dealing in general terms in relation
> to the subject, we are satisfied the doctrine contended for is not uni-
> versally true (VIII. Wheaton, 494).

In an English case arising under the Treaty of 1794, the
principle was distinctly recognized that they were to determine, by reasonable construction, *the intention of the treaty*
(Sutton *vs.* Sutton, 1 Rus. and M., 663). The question was,
whether American subjects who hold land in England were
to be considered, in respect of such lands, as aliens or subjects of Great Britain, or whether the War of 1812 had determined the Treaty of 1794. Sir J. Leach, the Master of
the Rolls, said : "The privileges of nations being reciprocally good, not only to actual possession of land, but to their
heirs and assigns, it is a reasonable construction that it was
the intention of the treaty that the operation of the treaty
should be permanent, and not depend upon the continuance
of a state of peace."

It is mentioned in Wharton's Digest, III. § 303, that
this decree was not appealed from. The last edition of
Wharton (1886) contains a valuable summary of the principles and cases bearing on the fishery questions under the
Treaties of 1783 and 1818 (III., pp. 38-57).

Mr. Blaine, in his "Twenty Years of Congress" (II., p.
617), alluded to

> The rather curious fact, apparently unknown or unnoticed by the
> negotiators of 1814, that as late as 1768 the law officers of the crown,
> under the last ministry of Lord Chatham (to whom was referred the

Treaty of 1686 with France, containing certain stipulations in relation
to the Newfoundland fisheries), gave as their opinion that such clauses
were permanent in their character, and that so far the treaty was valid,
notwithstanding subsequent war.

Mr. Blaine has kindly referred me to these cases in
Chalmer's opinions of eminent lawyers.

The question to which they relate arose upon the fifth
and sixth articles of the Treaty of Peace and Neutrality in
America, concluded between England and France, November 16, 1686, touching the neutral rights, conditions, and
disabilities of the inhabitants of each kingdom as regards
trade and fishing in the places possessed by them in America. On April 7, 1753, the attorney and solicitor-general,
Ryder and Murray, advised the Government of their opinion, without statement of their reasons, that " the said treaty
is now in force." On February 12, 1765, the attorney and
solicitor-general, Norton and De Grey, announced as their
opinion, without statement of their reasons, " that the said
treaty was not in force." On February 15, 1765, Sir
James Marriot, the advocate-general, gave his opinion that
the Treaty of Neutrality was a subsisting treaty ; and this
view is sustained in a very careful and elaborate argument, by broad and just considerations of good faith and
enlightened civilization, worthy of the noblest statesman-
ship and diplomacy of England.

His opinion showed that the treaties are in their nature
contracts, and are to be argued on the footing of obligations
which arise from contract expressed or necessarily implied,
and that the question of deciding the validity and exist-
ence of a public treaty is to be governed by the same
rules and reasonings applicable to other contracts. Touching their revival, from the very nature of the cause
claiming to operate which had suspended the force of the
convention, especially if the objects of good faith are con-
cerned in the revival, Sir James alluded to the fact that the
decision of such questions, in their age of negotiation,

must differ from the practices of barbarous nations with but partial notions of modern civilization; and that "in the present age, as war is commenced on different principles from the wars of antiquity, so it ends with different principles, in both more to the honor of humanity."

He showed that the public law of Europe abhors the spirit of ancient wars, and that war in these times is considered but as an appeal to the rest of the powers of Europe, and is but a temporary exertion of force to decide a point of interest which no human tribunal could determine, and he said :

Thus it is, in its nature, but a *suspense* of the other rights not in contest, which existed between the belligerent powers reciprocally, before the war ; when we reason, therefore, that a war being ended, the public reciprocal rights and obligations, not specially abrogated, but suspended, *emerge*, and acquire their former vigor and activity, the reasoning of it is just ; is so, because it is consistent with the relations, and arises out of the *nature* of things. We need not urge the necessity of particular stipulations, to revive such obligations ; it is the very essence and necessary idea of *reconciliation*, implied of course, if not declared, in every definitive treaty of pacification, that the commercial and friendly intercourse of the contracting powers is replaced in its former state.

. . . Such is the force of those exalted principles of public law which, in these happier ages of human society, restore their proper empire over the minds of men to good sense and good faith, with a force superior to the passions or prejudices of nations long accustomed to be rivals ; and such I conceive to be the law of Europe in its present state, which, whenever these doctrines, founded in reason and humanity, shall cease to prevail, will fall back into all the gloom of a barbarous condition of ignorance and despotism.

The war between England and France, which followed the revolution, suspended the commercial treaty of 1686, called the Treaty of Neutrality. The Treaty of Peace, concluded at Ryswick, 1697, takes no notice of it nominally, but revives it, by the general quality of a treaty, putting an end to the war by the strongest terms of a general comprehension, restoring the commerce of the two nations, reciprocally, to the state in which it existed before the war. . . .

I have the honor to submit that the Treaty of 1686 *may be insisted* upon as a subsisting treaty, not only because it is revived, by a strong implication of words and facts, but for that it may be *understood* to subsist because it never was abrogated.*

The exalted principles of public law declared in that masterly opinion of the Advocate-General in 1765, confirmatory of the opinion of Attorney-General Ryder and Solicitor-General Murray in 1753, that the fisheries article in the French and English treaty of 1686, while suspended by war, had been restored by the peace, apply in still greater force to the fisheries article in the Anglo-American Treaty of 1783, which was not only a treaty of peace but of separation, intended to settle definitely and permanently the boundaries, and the rights and liberties of the two nations in what had before been held by them in common. The War of 1812 suspended the exercise of the rights and liberties secured by the fisheries clause; and when the war was terminated by the Treaty of Ghent, that treaty, while taking no notice of the fisheries clause of 1783 nominally, " revived it by the general quality of a treaty putting an end to the war, and restoring the commerce of the two nations reciprocally to the state in which it existed before the war." Whether or not the weighty argument of Sir James Marriott was known to the British Commissioners at Ghent or at London, it will not be overlooked by Americans or by Englishmen in considering the question of the fisheries under the interesting circumstances of to-day.

Nor will they forget that the true doctrine of the effect of war on treaties, so clearly stated by Sir James in 1765, was recognized in the Parliamentary debates on the Peace of Amiens in 1802, between Great Britain, France, Spain, and Holland, by the great jurists of England, whose opinions seem to have been strangely ignored by the British Government, in its efforts to prove that our fishery rights

* Vol. II., pp. 344-355, of Opinions of Eminent Lawyers on Various Points of English Jurisprudence, chiefly Concerning the Colonies, Fisheries, and Commerce of Great Britain. By George Chalmers. London : Reed & Hunter, 1814.

under the Treaty of 1783 had been hopelessly annulled by the war of 1812.

In that Parliamentary debate, Lord Auckland said that it had been intimated by some that by the non-renewal of the Treaty of 1786 their right to cut logwood might be disputed, and in answer to that intimation Lord Auckland said:

> He had looked into the works of the first publicists on these subjects, and had corrected himself in a mistake still prevalent in the minds of many who state in an unqualified sense that all treaties between nations are annulled by war, and must be specially renewed if meant to be enforced on the return of peace. . . . But compacts not interrupted by the cause and effect of hostilities, such as the regulated exercise of a fishery on the respective coasts of the belligerent powers . . . are certainly not destroyed or injured by war.

The Earl of Carnarvon said in the same debate:

> War does not abrogate any right or interfere with the right, though it does with the exercise, but such as it professes to litigate by war.

Lord Ellenborough, Chief Justice of the Court of King's Bench,

> felt surprise that the non-renewal of treaties should have been urged as a serious objection to the definite treaty. . . . He was astonished to hear men of talent argue that the public law of Europe was a dead letter, because certain treaties were not renewed.

Lord Eldon, then High Chancellor of England; Lord Hawkesbury; the Earl of Liverpool, the Secretary of State for Foreign Affairs and late Prime Minister of England; Mr. Addington (Lord Sidmouth); Mr. Pitt, and Mr. Fox, all supported the same principles.*

* The opinions are referred to by Mr. John Quincy Adams in "The Fisheries and the Mississippi," p. 195, citing 23 Hansard, 1147, and are more fully quoted by Mr. C. A. Rodnay in his opinion on the fisheries, filed with, and endorsed by, President Monroe, November 4, 1818, cited in III. Wharton's International Digest, 1886, Sec. 303, pp. 44 and 45, from the Monroe MSS. in the Department of State.

THE GOVERNOR-GENERAL OF CANADA.

It may be regarded as a fortunate circumstance at this juncture that the Governor-General of Canada is a grandson of the great English Minister by whom our Revolutionary War was happily ended, on terms so fair and reasonable as forever to entitle the memory of Shelburne to the highest honor in both countries. His Excellency is familiar with the historic sketch by his brother, Lord Edmond Fitzmaurice, of the conduct of the peace negotiations by that statesman, the story of whose connection therewith has been of signal service in correcting the errors into which American historians had been misled, in regard to the secret devices of France and Spain to deprive us of the boundaries and the fisheries; to the secret mission of Rayneval to England to secure Shelburne's adhesion to their scheme; and to the great service rendered to the Republic by Benjamin Vaughan in hastening to Bowood at the request of Jay to counteract the designs of Rayneval, and to assist in engaging for the American Commissioners the confidence of Shelburne and a fair share of American rights.

Lord Lansdowne knows that at that time no peace was possible without the full recognition of our right to the fisheries. His Excellency without doubt values aright the inestimable service rendered by Shelburne to England, America, and the world, at the expense of a brief unpopularity. He will doubtless be the last person in Canada to wish to disturb the international friendship to which his illustrious ancestor so pre-eminently contributed, and which, as regards the fisheries, would probably never have been disturbed had the third article been allowed to stand as Shelburne approved it; and perhaps the surest guarantee for our mutual good-will will be found in a return to the terms of the treaty so conspicuously identified with his fame.

Concluding Suggestions.

It is not at all to be presumed that Lord Salisbury to whom, I may say in passing that we are all indebted for the ready courtesy with which he has permitted us to gather from the State-Paper Office of London the most interesting and important papers bearing on the peace negotiations, papers whose value we appreciate anew as we observe their bearing on the questions of to-day—it is not to be presumed that Lord Salisbury will decline to look at the rights we claim, not as privileges conceded to colonists, but as ancient rights won for Great Britain by American valour, of which we retained our share on the division of the empire, and of which, by well-established rules, we lost not an iota by the war. Nor is it to be presumed that Lord Salisbury will submit a question that so nearly concerns the honour and the interest of the British people to the decision of the Canadians, whose unwisdom has strained our relations, and who, even since the Halifax award, are not content; or that Lord Salisbury will on this occasion adopt the principle or the method which Mr. Greville attributes to Lord Palmerston, when he says that Lord Palmerston, in speaking of Lord Ashburton and his treaty with Webster, remarked: "We are all right, and the Americans all wrong. Never give up anything; insist on having the thing settled your own way, and if they won't consent, let it remain unsettled."

In view of the rights of our fishermen we cannot afford to let this thing remain unsettled; and it would seem as if the Canadians, unchecked by the Home Government, had put it in our power to end the grievances to which our fishermen are subjected.

In case Congress shall be clear, as the Retaliation Bill would seem to indicate, that Great Britain has violated Article I. of the Treaty of 1818; and that the United States is therefore entitled, under the rule stated by Madison and established by her own precedent, to abrogate that article,

and to fall back upon the original rights and liberties of
the United States in the Newfoundland fisheries at the
division of the empire in 1783, as defined by Article III.
of the Treaty of Peace. Congress may be disposed to
consider the expediency of embodying their views on this
point in the Retaliation Act, or in a separate act, so that
the future negotiations for an amicable adjustment of the
pending difficulties may not be hampered nor thwarted by
the pretence, heretofore made, that the rights claimed by our
Government for American fishermen are denied to them by
the third article of the Treaty of 1818, which the British
have themselves violated.

Should this conclusion be approved by Congress, it
would almost follow the preamble and enacting clause of
the Act abrogating the treaties with France (July 7, 1798)
should it declare that, inasmuch as the third article has been
repeatedly violated on the part of the British Government,
and the just claims of the United States for reparation of
the injuries so committed have been refused, and their at-
tempts to negotiate an amicable settlement of the same have
failed, and under the authority of the British Government
a course of treatment is still pursued against the fishermen
of the United States, infracting the said article and hostile
to the rights of a free and independent nation, it is enacted
by Congress that the United States are of right freed and
exonerated from the stipulations of the said article, and
that the same shall not henceforth be regarded as legally obligatory on the Government or citizens of the United States.

While Congress may approve the propriety and necessity of such an act, it may at the same time deem it proper
to postpone the taking effect of such an enactment, so long
as a reasonable hope may be entertained that Great Britain
will voluntarily do full and ample justice to our fishermen ;
and Congress may deem it wise to leave it to the President,
as in the Retaliation Bill, to give it effect in his discretion.

It is desirable that not only Great Britain, but all the
world, should see that, while resolved to maintain our rights

and protect our fishermen, and to end at once and forever the petty vexations to which they have been subjected and which now threaten the international peace, we sincerely desire, if possible, to preserve and improve our friendly relations with Great Britain and her dependencies on this continent.

Recalling the prominent part so ably borne by you at Geneva in the tribunal which, to the admiration of Europe, closed amicably the Alabama question, we may hail as of good omen your presence in the Senate at this time, when England and America both desire the closing of the fisheries dispute : and trusting that we may soon have an early and satisfactory end of this business on the basis of the original rights of both countries,

I am, very respectfully and faithfully yours,

JOHN JAY.

191 SECOND AVENUE, NEW YORK,
February 22, 1887.

www.ingramcontent.com/pod-product-compliance
Lightning Source LLC
Chambersburg PA
CBHW021643270326
41931CB00008B/1149